Editor
Sara Connolly

Managing Editor
Ina Massler Levin, M.A.

Illustrator
Tracy Reynolds

Cover Artist
Denise Bauer

Art Production Manager
Kevin Barnes

Imaging
James Edward Grace
Rosa C. See

Publisher
Mary D. Smith, M.S. Ed.

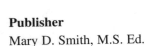

Grades 1-2

Readers' Theater

Sight Words

Ideal for Fluency Practice

Retold by

Maureen Gerard, Ph.D.

Teacher Created Resources, Inc.
6421 Industry Way
Westminster, CA 92683
www.teachercreated.com

ISBN 13: 978-1-4206-3068-8

©*2006 Teacher Created Resources, Inc.*
Reprinted, 2007
Made in U.S.A.

Table of Contents

Introduction

The Connection between Fluency and Readers' Theater

Performance reading in the form of readers' theater is a motivating, interesting, and exciting way to include oral reading in the curriculum. Repeated reading in readers' theater is a powerful tool for developing reading fluency, particularly in the elementary grades. As teachers, we have noticed that children who read aloud in reading groups often skip ahead to preview their own passage and fail to read along with the other students. Or, the students will try to read so fast, little understanding or comprehension is possible. In contrast, oral reading in readers' theater helps to build confidence in reluctant readers. Oral reading in readers' theater strengthens decoding skills. It connects spoken and written language. It boosts comprehension, and it provides accurate, informal assessment of reading development. It is a simple educational tool for reading authentic literature in repeated practice readings that are multiple and purposeful. No costumes, props, or scenery are required unless the students and teacher wish to include them in the performance. Without movement and performance paraphernalia, children have only one attribute to make their performance meaningful and convincing…their voices.

Fluency is the ability to read quickly and accurately while at the same time using expression and proper phrasing. Fluency is particularly important when considering young children just learning to read or readers just beginning to read English. Those students who expend so much effort decoding words letter by letter decrease their understanding of the material because their attention and energy is not focused on finding meaning and sense in the text. You will notice this when, after listening to a struggling reader, you find that the student does not understand what he or she has just read.

Children who read more fluently use their energy and attention to focus on the meaning of the print. They comprehend what they read. The fluent reader has enough attention in reserve to make connections between the text and his or her own background knowledge, which gives the reader a much richer understanding of the material. When oral reading of text is more fluent, and sounds like natural speech, children are better able to pull from their own prior knowledge and experiences for comprehension.

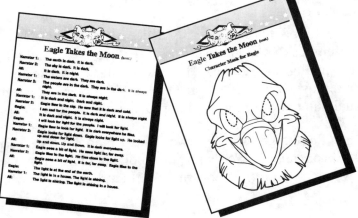

Introduction *(cont.)*

The Connection between Fluency and Readers' Theater *(cont.)*

Reading fluency does not develop quickly. As adults we have all experienced the need to reread something that we did not understand at first reading. It could have been a technical manual, a cooking recipe, or a newspaper article, but through rereading, we were able to pull the meaning from the words. Many children balk at reading a selection over again. The struggling readers, who need it most, may be particularly unmotivated. If told to read silently, these students often pretend to read, and the more advanced readers are bored by the whole notion of going through the text a second time when they feel that they understood it the first time.

The readers' theater scripts in this book include parts for several children to read together. The students are also participating in a limited form of paired reading, which is another proven fluency strategy. In paired reading, a stronger reader reads aloud with a weaker reader. By listening to the fluent reader, the weaker reader learns how the readers' voice, expression, and phrasing help to make sense of the print.

Readers' theater is not only effective in developing reading fluency, it is capable of transforming a class into excited readers. It is one activity within the school day where the struggling readers do not stand out. With teacher support and repeated practice, all students can read their lines with accuracy and expression and gain confidence in their own reading abilities. It is a simple tool that covers multiple objectives in reading instruction.

Sight Word Practice

Children come to school to learn to read and write. Every teacher wants to teach all of his or her students to read and write well. However, not every child learns in the same way or at the same rate. Some children will arrive at school with a rich understanding of literacy and others will come with little background knowledge of print, letters, or language. Some students will learn words best using phonetic decoding, stringing together letter shapes with sounds to form words. Others will rely on visual clues to recall a word by its context or shape.

Readers' theater scripts for sight word practice allow the teacher to provide a series of lessons and oral reading opportunities to children of varying reading levels and different learning styles in a whole class setting or in a small group setting. The readers' theater scripts in this book reinforce the sight words which children must recognize automatically. Sight words are repeated to develop visual memory, improve visual-auditory perception, and provide repeated, meaningful practice with sight words.

Sight words are those high frequency words which do not necessarily decode and which must be read by children with automaticity. Words for this book are taken from Dr. Fry's 300 Instant Sight Words. The words used were chosen for the coherence of the trickster tale while maintaining rank on Dr. Fry's list.

Introduction *(cont.)*

Trickster Tales

Trickster tales are part of a body of traditional folklore and mythological literature including stories, songs, and poems that have been passed along through oral storytelling. Trickster stories and their mythical characters have been present worldwide since the earliest times. The authors of these folktales are unknown because of decades of telling and retelling the stories. The timeless appeal of trickster tales has made them memorable from generation to generation. And, many cultures still maintain a vital, strong tradition of oral storytelling that includes trickster tales. Trickster tales especially lend themselves to multiple repetitions and simple word combinations. These delightful stories invite active audience participation which makes them ideal story matter for readers' theater scripts.

Animal tales have entertained and delighted children down through the ages. Animal tricksters are fun, appealing characters who challenge the status quo, cross moral and social boundaries, or simply play the fool. The trickster questions the way that the world works and the organization of life by his playfulness and his liberties with language. The outlandish but remarkable trickster blunders his way into outrageous predicaments, learns life's lessons "the hard way," grows into understanding the natural order of life, and finally, becomes the story's hero. He is at once troublemaker and champion. He expresses so much of the human condition in his repertoire of tricks and disguises. Like the trickster, we blunder, learn from our mistakes, and try on an array of social masks and personas.

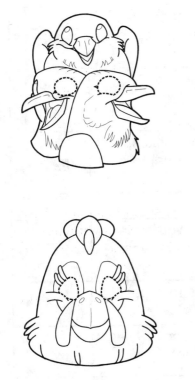

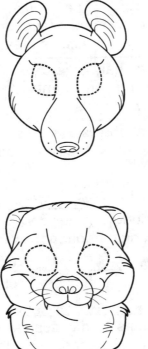

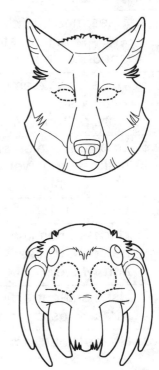

Standards in the Language Arts

The National Council of Teachers of English together with the International Reading Association published a framework of standards for the English Language Arts in 1996. In 1999, Mid-Continent Research for Education and Learning published skill specific benchmarks to add detail and specificity to the national language arts standards already developed by NCTE and IRA. The McREL benchmarks were used to develop the lessons in this book. The chart below shows the McREL standards for language arts for grades K-3. The checks indicate the standards that are addressed in readers' theater.

Standard 5: Uses the general skills and strategies of the reading process	
1. Understands that print conveys meaning (i.e., knows that printed letters and words represent spoken language)	✓
2. Understands how print is organized and read (e.g., identifies front and back covers, title page, author, and illustrator; follows words from left to right and from top to bottom; knows the significance of spaces between words, knows the difference between letters, words, and sentences; understands the use of capitalization and punctuation as text boundaries)	✓
3. Creates mental images from pictures and print	✓
4. Uses meaning clues (e.g., pictures, picture captions, title, cover, headings, story structure, story topic) to aid comprehension and make predictions about content (e.g., action, events, character's behavior)	
5. Uses basic elements of phonetic analysis (e.g., common letter/sound relationships, beginning and ending consonants, vowel sounds, blends, word patterns) to decode unknown words	✓
6. Uses basic elements of structural analysis (e.g., syllables, basic prefixes, suffixes, root words, compound words, spelling patterns, contractions) to decode unknown words	✓
7. Uses a picture dictionary to determine word meaning	✓
8. Understands level-appropriate sight words and vocabulary (e.g., words for persons, places, things, actions; high-frequency words, such as *said*, *was*, and *where*)	✓
9. Uses self-correction strategies (e.g., searches for cues, identifies miscues, rereads, asks for help)	✓
10. Reads aloud familiar stories, poems, and passages with fluency and expression (e.g., rhythm, flow, meter, tempo, pitch, tone, intonation)	✓

Standards in the Language Arts *(cont.)*

Standard 6: Uses reading skills and strategies to understand and interpret a variety of literary texts	
1. Uses reading skills and strategies to understand a variety of familiar literary passages and texts (e.g., fairy tales, folktales, fiction, nonfiction, legends, fables, myths, poems, nursery rhymes, picture books, predictable books)	✓
2. Knows setting, main characters, main events, sequence, and problems in stories	✓
3. Makes simple inferences regarding the order of events and possible outcomes	✓
4. Knows the main ideas or theme of a story	✓
5. Relates stories to personal experiences (e.g., events, characters, conflicts, themes)	✓

Standard 7: Uses reading skills and strategies to understand and interpret a variety of informational texts	
1. Uses reading skills and strategies to understand a variety of informational texts (e.g., written directions, signs, captions, warning labels, informational books)	
2. Understands the main idea and supporting details of simple expository information	✓
3. Summarizes information found in texts (e.g., retells in own words)	✓
4. Relates new information to prior knowledge and experience	✓

Preparation for Trickster Tales Readers' Theater

How to use these reading lessons and Trickster Tale Readers' Theater scripts

The outline given below is a suggested plan for using the readers' theater scripts with the lesson plans presented in this book. You can plan to use one trickster tale script each week or use several scripts in one week. You should adapt these ideas to fit your classroom schedule.

Lesson 1

- Teach Lesson Plan 1 for sight word practice (pages 13–14).

- Pre-read the trickster tale script that you have selected with your students in one of the following ways:

  1. Read the script aloud to the whole class using an overhead copy of the trickster tale script.

  2. Read the script aloud to the whole class in Shared Reading with each student reading from a personal copy of the trickster tale script.

  3. Have students form small groups and read the scripts for Guided Reading. (Guided reading groups are small groups of children who meet with the teacher to read as the teacher guides the reading activity.)

  4. Partner two students for Buddy Reading—two students partnered to read the trickster tale script by alternating parts.

  5. Partner two students for Paired Reading—two students reading the trickster tale script together at the same time.

- Have students practice their scripts as homework.

Lesson 2

- Teach Lesson Plan 2 for more sight word practice (pages 17–18)

- Practice reading the trickster tale script you have selected with your students in one of these ways:

  1. Have the whole class practice while reading from individual copies of a script.

  2. Have the whole class practice in small groups, doing guided reading in "performance groups."

  3. Have small groups do independent practice reading in "performance groups."

- Have students practice their scripts as homework.

Preparation for Trickster Tales Readers' Theater *(cont.)*

Lesson 3

- Teach Lesson Plan 3 for observing punctuation for fluent reading (pages 20–21).

- Continue practice reading of the trickster tale script in one of the following ways:

    1. whole class reading from individual copies of a trickster tale script
    2. small group, guided reading in "performance groups"
    3. small group, independent practice reading

- Create character masks for performance day.

- Have students practice their scripts as homework

Lesson 4

- Teach Lesson Plan 4 for developing vocabulary (pages 22–23).

- Continue practice reading of the trickster tale script in one of the following ways:

    1. whole class reading from individual copies of a trickster tale script
    2. small group, guided reading in "performance groups"
    3. small group, independent practice reading

- Assign word study activities from Lesson Plan 4 using new vocabulary words.

- Have students practice their scripts as homework

Lesson 5

- Teach Lesson Plan 5 on observing stress in oral reading (page 24).

- Review director hints for performance with the students in a final practice reading.

- Performance Day!

Preparation for Trickster Tales Readers' Theater *(cont.)*

Materials

- copies of the readers' theater scripts for each student

- overhead transparency of the trickster tale script for whole class instruction

- highlighters, pencils to mark each individual student script

Preparation

- Photocopy the trickster tale scripts.

  (Optional) Make two copies of the script so that each student has one script for school practice and one for home practice.

- Highlight each individual part; this may be done by the teacher in advance or by the student on his or her own copy of the script.

  (Optional) Students may want to use character masks while performing. Photocopy the character masks to be used in the performance on cardstock, one mask per character.

Optional

- crayons or markers for each student to color the cardstock character mask

- scissors for each student to cut out the cardstock mask (both the outline and the eyes) of the character he/she will portray

- craft sticks

- glue to attach one craft stick to the back of each mask

Readers' Theater Director Hints

Preparing

- Have the students underline lightly in pencil on their scripts all of the directions for any movements and gestures for the character in either the printed stage directions or other readers' speeches. Direct them to write in extra stage directions in the margin as they are developed in your classroom script practice.

- Help the students to read unknown vocabulary (refer to Lesson Plan 4, pages 22–23) and to correctly pronounce words that he or she does not know.

- Encourage the students to try out faces, gestures, and movements. Ask the students to think about how the character would stand and move.

- Direct the students to practice their parts at home in a mirror to watch their faces and movements.

Rehearsing

Help your students to get more vocal power by checking their breathing. To do this, the students must place their hands on their stomachs and inhale. If the students are actually filling their lungs, their hands will be pushed out as they inhale. The diaphragm muscle gives the lungs more room to expand by pushing down on the stomach. If their hands move in and the stomach gets tighter, it means the students are filling only the top parts of their lungs. To help your students stand up straight, ask them to imagine a wire attached to their chests, pulling straight up to the ceiling.

- Direct the students to hold their script steady, making sure they don't cover their mouths. If the student can't see people in the front row of the audience, the script is too high.

- Tell the students to try to look up often. The students should keep their heads still and only move their eyes.

- Tell the students to s-p-e-a-k s-l-o-w-l-y and c-l-e-a-r-l-y and l-o-u-d-l-y.

- Speak with feeling.

- Narrators control the story! They must be sure to give all the characters enough time to say each line and to make each gesture. Generally, the narrators are speaking to the audience.

- Characters bring the story to life! Direct the students to be in character even when not speaking, and to listen to and react to the other characters' lines.

Readers' Theater Director Hints *(cont.)*

Performing

Performance day is here! Direct your students to:

- Stop speaking while the audience laughs.

- Ignore anyone who might walk in after the performance starts.

- Don't look up at anyone in the audience.

- Pretend that any mistakes were intended.

- Try to leave anything you drop on the ground until the audience is looking somewhere else.

Trickster Tales Lesson Plans

Lesson Plan 1: Sight Word Practice

McRel Standards Benchmark 5.1, 5.2, 5.3, 5.5, 5.6, 5.7, 5.8, 5.9, 5.10, 6.1, 6.2, 6.3, 6.5, 6.6.

Objectives

- Successful practice of sight words to expand sight reading vocabulary and increase automaticity in reading sight words.
- To reinforce visual memory, letter and vowel identification, letter formation and sequence, and to improve visual-auditory perception.

Materials

copies of Sight Word Practice Form, page 16

Procedure

As students are given the opportunity to read and reread the trickster tale scripts several times, the fluency and automaticity of sight word reading will improve. However, there will be sight words at which each child may pause or hesitate when reading. These are the sight words for which additional repetition and practice is most needed.

1. Begin by explaining to the students that sight words are words which they should be able to read quickly, easily, with no thought, by "sight." Explain also that these words are repeated over and over in their trickster tale scripts for added practice.

2. Explain that some sight words will be more difficult for the students to learn than others. These will be the sight words for extra practice.

3. Listen to each student read his or her role in guided reading groups. (Guided reading groups are small groups of children who meet with the teacher to read as the teacher guides the reading activity.) Note which sight words in the script are the most challenging for each student.

4. Give students directions for practice exercises for these challenging sight words. The Sight Word Practice exercises are designed to allow a student to write his or her own new word lesson.

5. Allow the students to play the role of instructor with the Sight Word Practice exercise. Trading exercises with a fellow student will increase confidence with the sight word list.

Trickster Tales Lesson Plans *(cont.)*

Lesson Plan 1: Sight Word Practice *(cont.)*

English Language Learner Support

Students learning English as a second language will require additional practice and repetition with many more of the sight words in the trickster tale scripts. No more than approximately five words should be given to these students for practice exercises at one time so that they are not overwhelmed by the new words. Retention will be improved with auditory reinforcement. Students should orally repeat the sight words throughout the practice exercises to strengthen their retention.

- Start the practice exercise by saying the sight word several times.

- Intersperse the writing on the practice exercise with rereading the completed portions aloud to allow a manual rest.

- Request that the students write the word in the air while they say the word, naming each letter as they make the air motions and then repeating the word once they are finished writing it in the air.

- End the practice exercise by saying the sight word several times again.

Trickster Tales Lesson Plans *(cont.)*

Lesson Plan 1: Sight Word Practice *(cont.)*

Tracing the Word

Tracing the word allows the student to be introduced to the new sight word in a non-threatening manner. The student becomes familiar with the letters making up the word and their sequence. There is the secondary benefit of letter formation practice.

Finding the Box

Asking a child to find the box that the word fits into allows the child to focus on the entire word shape, or gestalt, of the word. This activity forces a child to think about how the letters fit against each other—are there letters that go above or below the line, and do those upward and downward letters go at the beginning of the word or at the end?

Circling the Word Letters from the Alphabet

This seemingly simple activity is important on several levels. It reinforces alphabet sequence while providing an exercise in visual matching. Most importantly, it helps a child realize that language is manageable. Every word is going to be formed from these same 26 letters—regardless of the number of letters a word contains and what the letters are. It develops within a child a sense that language is a code with a finite number of pieces. New words will be assemblages of the code pieces.

Filling in the Missing Letters

Requiring a child to fill in missing letters allows a child to develop an awareness of letter sequence without being overwhelmed by the task. It reinforces the understanding that every letter is needed to make up a word and that the letter must appear in a particular order. It aids in spelling mastery as well as providing the secondary benefit of letter formation practice.

Circling the Vowels

As with circling the word letters from the alphabet, this activity is important on several levels. Obviously it reinforces vowel identification, but it also helps to develop the sense that the language code (reading) has rules. Every word requires at least one vowel. Although circling the vowels may not seem that important when sight words are introduced, familiarity with vowels will help during later phonics exercises, syllabication, and spelling.

Fixing Spelling Errors

During this exercise, a child is given the authority to be the "doctor." It is a given that the word is spelled incorrectly. It is up to the child to fix it. By having to fix the word several times, each time identifying a different error, proper spelling is reinforced. To many students, the idea of fixing something is what maintains their interest. They enjoy crossing out wrong letters and inserting correct ones. In addition, this exercise aids in developing editing skills. Checking that one has used the correct vowel and letter formation (b versus d, for example), provides practice for the types of things that a child will look for when he or she is self-correcting his or her own work later on. A teacher may want to instruct the children on the use of the caret (^), the editing symbol for the insertion of a letter, at this time. Rewriting the word entirely is optional.

Trickster Tales Lesson Plans *(cont.)*

Sight Word Practice Form

Name: _____   Date: _____

(write the new word here)

Trace the word.

(Write the new word three times so it can be traced.)

Find the box the word fits into.

(Make three boxes. Only one box should fit your new word shape.)

Circle the letters from the alphabet found in the new word.

a b c d e f g h i j k l m n o p q r s t u v w x y z

Fill in the missing letters.

(Write the word four times, leaving out different letters each time.)

Circle the vowels in the new word. The vowels are: a, e, i, o, u.

(Write the new word.)

Fix these words so they spell the new word correctly.

(Write the word four times. Spell the word incorrectly each time so it can be fixed.)

Trickster Tales Lesson Plans
Lesson Plan 2: More Sight Word Practice

McRel Standards Benchmark 5.1, 5.2, 5.3, 5.5, 5.6, 5.7, 5.8, 5.9, 5.10, 6.1, 6.2, 6.3, 6.5, 6.6.

Objectives

- Successful practice of sight words to expand sight reading vocabulary and increase automaticity in reading sight words.

- To reinforce visual memory, letter and vowel identification, letter formation and sequence, and to improve visual-auditory perception.

Materials

- copies of My Sight Word Flashcards, page 19, one copy for each student on cardstock

- copies of Sight Word Flashcards, pages 77–96

Procedure

As students are given the opportunity to read and reread the trickster tale scripts several times, the fluency and automaticity of sight word reading will improve. However, there will be sight words at which each child may pause or hesitate when reading. These are the sight words for which additional repetition and practice is most needed.

1. Begin by explaining to the students that sight words are words which they should be able to read quickly, with no thought, by "sight." Explain also that these words are repeated over and over in their trickster tale scripts for added practice.

2. Explain that some sight words will be more difficult for the students to learn than others. These will be the words for extra practice.

3. Listen to each student read his or her role in guided reading groups. (Guided reading groups are small groups of children who meet with the teacher to read as the teacher guides the reading activity.) Note which sight words in the script are the most challenging for each student.

4. Give students directions for completing the My Sight Word Flashcards page for these challenging sight words. The flashcard blanks are designed to allow a student to write his or her own new word flashcard.

Trickster Tales Lesson Plans *(cont.)*

Lesson Plan 2: More Sight Word Practice

Procedure *(cont.)*

5. Allow the students to play the role of instructor with the Sight Word Flashcards to help them to gain mastery of the words. Trading flashcards and practicing with a fellow student will increase confidence and automatic reading with the sight word flashcards.

English Language Learner Support

Students learning English as a second language will require additional practice and repetition with many more of the sight words in the trickster tale scripts. No more than approximately five words should be given to these students for flashcard practice at one time so that they are not overwhelmed by the volume of new words. Retention will be improved with auditory reinforcement. Add five words from the preprinted flashcards to the student's personal Sight Word Flashcards. Allowing the English language learning students to play the role of instructor with the Sight Word Flashcards will help them to gain mastery of the words. Trading flashcards and practicing with a more advanced reader will increase confidence and automatic reading with the sight word flashcards.

Trickster Tales Lesson Plans *(cont.)*

My Sight Word Flashcards

Trickster Tales Lesson Plans *(cont.)*

Lesson Plan 3: Instructing the Fluency Objectives (Observing Punctuation, Using Intonation)

McRel Standards Benchmark: 5.1, 5.2, 5.3, 5.5, 5.6, 5.7, 5.8, 5.9, 5.10, 6.1, 6.2, 6.3, 6.5, 6.6.

Objective

- Students will read the script, pausing to observe punctuation and using appropriate voice pitch and intonation for the punctuation.

Materials

- pencils

Procedure

When parts have been assigned and performance groups formed for the readers' theater, meet with each group as a guided reading group. Explain to the students in the guided reading group that a major goal for readers' theater is for the students to become "unglued" from the words on the page and to be able to read the words quickly and accurately "by sight" as if talking to a friend.

Early readers need to know how to read punctuation correctly when they encounter different marks.

1. First, students need to recognize and differentiate the punctuation marks /? !/. Have students look for and circle the punctuation marks in pencil on their own copies of the trickster tale script.

2. Demonstrate reading with proper intonation using this line from the Fox, Snake, and the Birds script:

   Oh, if only I could fly. I would be the greatest fox of all.

   Explain to the students that your voice goes "down" at the end of a sentence with a period.

3. Point out to the students where the end punctuation is for each line so that they may check their own work from step 1. Repeat the reading using the different end punctuation of a question mark and an exclamation mark. Ask the students what they heard in your voice quality for each type of punctuation. Explain to students that your voice goes "up" with a question mark and expresses surprise, dismay, or pleasure at the exclamation point.

Trickster Tales Lesson Plans *(cont.)*

Lesson Plan 3: Instructing the Fluency Objectives (Observing Punctuation, Using Intonation) *(cont.)*

Procedure *(cont.)*

4. Have students reread their lines of the script especially observing the end punctuation.

   Complete the practice reading of the script observing and marking for punctuation and intonation.

English Language Learner Support

Students who are learning English as a second language will benefit from modeling of reading to observe punctuation and intonation. Echo reading will help those students to change stress and pitch, observe pauses, and chunk phrases of the text together. Choose a part from the script and read one phrase or sentence at a time as the student follows along on his or her script. Have the student echo read the same phrase or sentence exactly as you read it. Point out the part where you raise your voice at the end of a question. Read an exclamation point with strong emotion. Point out your pause at a comma, at the end of a sentence, and at the end of a paragraph. Have students explain where they have difficulties following your lead. Then have the students point out the changes they must follow in your stress, pitch, pauses, and chunking for fluent reading. Finally, have pairs of students reread together chorally or echo read with each other after you have modeled this for them.

Trickster Tales Lesson Plans *(cont.)*
Lesson Plan 4: Developing Vocabulary

McRel Standards Benchmark: 5.1, 5.2, 5.3, 5.5, 5.6, 5.7, 5.8, 5.9, 5.10, 6.1, 6.2, 6.3, 6.5, 6.6.

Objectives

- Students will identify unknown vocabulary words from the readers' theater script.
- Students will use a variety of context clues to learn unknown vocabulary words from the readers' theater script.

Materials

- index cards
- colored markers

Procedure

1. Provide each student with a copy of one of the trickster tale scripts and read the parts aloud as a whole class. (You may want to first read the script to the students as they follow along. As you read the script aloud, use varying voice and expression for the different characters.)

2. Ask the students to name the words in the script which are new, unknown words for them.

3. Record all new vocabulary words found by the students on to index cards. Staple or tape the cards to the classroom word wall. (The classroom word wall is a learning tool for organizing new words that the students learn to read and write. Teachers can create a word wall on a chalkboard, bulletin board, or wall space by stapling or taping the letters of the alphabet in order to serve as headings to group the new words together.) Alternately, you record the new vocabulary words onto chart paper or onto the chalkboard.

4. Use the newly created list for vocabulary word study. For example:

   - Use a colored marker to underline roots and affixes, as well as to list other words students know that look like, sound like, or have similar meanings to the new vocabulary words.

   - Use the new vocabulary word list to play the game "I'm Thinking of...." Begin by saying "I'm thinking of a word that means the same as *yelled loudly* or *howled*." Call on a student and have him or her respond with a complete sentence, such as "Are you thinking of *bellowed*?" Answer, "Yes, I am thinking of *bellowed*," as you check off or erase the word. The "I'm Thinking of..." game allows for the definition of words, and meaningful repetition and practice.

   - Choose a word that contains several consonants and at least two vowels, such as *government*, and have students "shake it up" to form new words such as *greet* and *gone*.

Trickster Tales Lesson Plans *(cont.)*

Lesson Plan 4: Developing Vocabulary *(cont.)*

ELL Support

Students who are low-level readers or ELL Students would benefit greatly from hearing the script read fluently as they read along with their script. You may want these students to listen to an audio recording of the trickster tale at a listening center. You may also want to provide time outside of your readers' theater lesson to allow them extra practice in paired reading with the recording.

Trickster Tales Lesson Plans *(cont.)*

Lesson Plan 5: Developing Vocabulary: Instructing the Fluency Objectives (Observing Stress in Oral Reading)

McRel Standards Benchmark: 5.1, 5.2, 5.3, 5.5, 5.6, 5.7, 5.8, 5.9, 5.10, 6.1, 6.2, 6.3, 6.6, 6.5.

Objective

- Students will read the script using appropriate voice pitch and stress for conveying meaning.

Procedure

1. Demonstrate reading with different stress placed on the words in a sentence. Ask students how the stress changes the meaning of the sentence.

   Oh, if only I could **fly**. I would be the greatest fox of all.

   Oh, if only I could fly. I would be the **greatest** fox of all.

   Oh, if only I could fly. I would be the greatest fox of all.

   Oh, if only I could fly. I would be the greatest fox of **all**.

2. Have students reread their lines of the script placing the stress on different words in the sentence. Complete the practice reading of the script observing and marking lightly with a pencil for end punctuation, intonation, and best stress.

English Language Learners Support

Students who are learning English as a second language will benefit from modeling of reading to observe punctuation and intonation. Echo reading will help these students to change stress and pitch, observe pauses, and chunk phrases of the text together. Choose a part from the script and read one phrase or sentence at a time as the student follows along on their script. Have the student echo read the same phrase or sentence exactly as you read it. Point out the part where you raise your voice at the end of a question. Read an exclamation point with strong emotion. Point out your pause at a comma, at the end of a sentence, and at the end of a paragraph. Have students explain where they have difficulties following your lead. Then have the students point out the changes they must follow in your stress, pitch, pauses, and chunking for fluent reading. Finally, have pairs of students reread together chorally or echo read with each other after you have modeled this for them.

Fox, Snake, and the Birds

Roles

Narrator 1 & 2, Fox, Snake, Flock of Birds, All

Trickster Tale Summary

The fox is often depicted as a trickster character trying to outwit his prey. In this tale, Fox foolishly tries to be like the birds. He tries to fly and dance like the birds only to tumble to the ground. He rolls through the dust and becomes grey and dirty instead of lovely red. The tale tells children how the fox got his color.

Sight Words

The sight words in this list are the words repeated throughout this trickster tale.

a	after	all	and	are	at	be	but	by	back
can	call	color	could	did	down	don't	for	from	find
found	fast	fly	funny	got	he	his	I	if	in
is	into	like	leave	left	me	must	may	not	now
old	one	only	out	please	ran	right	sing	the	their
they	to	too	thank	took	us	want	with	you	

Vocabulary Words

The words in this list may be new words for your students. Review the list before reading the readers' theater script with your students.

birds	feather	proud	silly	twitched	winced
curious	flock	rude	snake	trouble	

Characters

Narrator 1 _____

Narrator 2 _____

Fox _____

Snake _____

Flock of Birds _____

All _____

Fox, Snake, and the Birds

Narrator 1:   Fox. Red, red fox.

Narrator 2:   Fox is curious.

All: Fox is curious. Fox is curious about many things.

Narrator 1:   Fox sticks his nose into Snake's hole.

All: Ouch! Ouch!   Fox gets his nose bitten. Snake bites his nose.

Narrator 2:   Fox looks for Snake. Fox finds trouble. Snake is trouble.

All: Fox is curious. Watch out, Fox!

Narrator 1:   Fox finds a flock of birds. Fox is curious.

Fox: How do these birds fly? Oh, if only I could fly. I would be the greatest fox of all.

Narrator 2:   Fox calls out to the flock of birds. Fox is curious.

Fox: How do you fly, birds? Please, please let me join you. Please let me try.

Narrator 1:   Snake is trouble. Watch out, Fox!

All: Snake is trouble. Watch out, Fox!

Snake: *(To the audience)* This s-s-silly fox wants to fly like the birds.

Flock of Birds: This silly fox wants to fly like us. This silly fox wants to fly like us.. *(laughing at Fox)* Ca-ha! Ca-ha! Ca-ha ha ha!

Snake: *(To the audience)* This s-s-silly fox wants to fly like the birds.

Flock of Birds: This silly fox wants to fly like us. This silly fox wants to fly like us. *(laughing at Fox)* Ca-ha! Ca-ha! Ca-ha ha ha!

Snake: You can fly, Fox! You can fly like the birds.

Flock of Birds: You may join us. You may fly with us.

Fox: Thank you! Thank you! I want to fly, too!

Flock of Birds: You may join us. You may fly with us.

Fox: I want to join you. I want to fly, too!

Fox, Snake, and the Birds *(cont.)*

Flock of Birds: *(laughing at Fox)* Ca-ha! Ca-ha! Ca-ha ha ha! He wants to fly, too! He wants to fly, too!

Snake: You can. You can fly, too.

Fox: Thank you! Thank you!

Narrator 1: The flock of birds took feathers from their left wings. They stuck the feathers in Fox.

Narrator 2: Fox winced. Fox twitched.

All: He winced and twitched. He winced and twitched.

Snake: Now you can fly, Fox. You are ready to fly.

Flock of Birds: *(laughing at Fox)* Ca-ha! Ca-ha! Ca-ha ha ha! Now you can fly! Now you can fly!

Narrator 1: The birds flew into the sky.

Narrator 2: Fox followed into the sky.

All: The birds flew into the sky. Fox followed into the sky.

Narrator 1: Fox flapped. He tipped. Fox flipped. Fox fell.

Fox: Wait! Wait! Don't leave me! Please, don't leave me behind!

Flock of Birds: We must help. We must help Fox.

Narrator 2: The flock of birds pulled feathers from their right wings. They stuck the feathers in Fox.

Narrator 1: Fox winced. Fox twitched.

All: He winced and twitched. He winced and twitched.

Flock of Birds: *(laughing at Fox)* Ca-ha! Ca-ha! Ca-ha ha ha! This silly fox wants to be like us.

Fox: Now I am just right! I can fly as well as the rest of you. Now I am the greatest fox of all!

Fox, Snake, and the Birds *(cont.)*

All:	Fox was rude. Fox was proud. Fox thinks he is the greatest fox of all.
Narrator 1:	The birds flew into the sky.
Narrator 2:	Fox followed into the sky.
All:	The birds flew into the sky. Fox followed into the sky.
Narrator 1:	Fox flapped. He tipped. Fox flipped.
Fox:	Carry me! Please, carry me!
Narrator 1:	The birds did not carry Fox.
Narrator 2:	The birds took back their feathers from Fox. One by one.
Narrator 1:	One by one, they took their feathers back.
Narrator 2:	Fox fell. Fox fell through the air. Fox fell straight down.
All:	Fox fell. He fell through the air. Fox fell straight down.
Fox:	Help! Help! Catch me! Catch me!
Narrator 1:	Fox fell fast. He fell into the mud.
Fox:	I am falling! Catch me! I am falling!
Flock of Birds:	*(laughing at Fox)* Ca-ha! Ca-ha! Ca-ha ha ha! This silly fox wants to be like us.
Narrator 2:	Fox heard laughing. He heard the birds laughing.
All:	Fox tripped. Fox fell. Fox rolled in the mud.
Narrator 1:	Fox went home muddy. He went home covered with dirt.
All:	Fox is rude. Fox is proud. Fox thinks he is the greatest of all. Fox is the color of mud now.

Fox, Snake, and the Birds *(cont.)*

Character Mask for Fox

Fox, Snake, and the Birds *(cont.)*

Character Mask for Snake

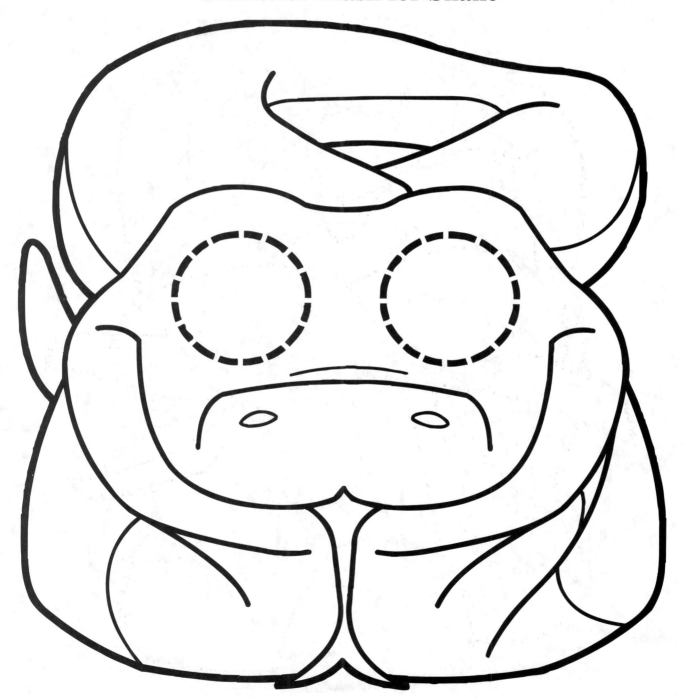

Fox, Snake, and the Birds *(cont.)*

Character Mask for Flock of Birds

Mouse Tricks the Crocodiles

Roles

Narrator 1 & 2, Mouse, Crocodile, All

Trickster Tale Summary

A little mouse is the trickster of this tale. Wanting to get across the river and continue on his journey through the jungle, the mouse comes up with a clever idea to make a bridge across the river. The mouse calls the crocodiles living in the river to come to the bank to be counted for the king. In order to properly count the crocodiles for the king, the mouse tells the crocodiles they must line up side by side from one bank of the river all the way to the other bank of the river. The crocodiles line up and mouse tricks them all as he hops across the backs of the ferocious creatures, counting aloud until he reaches the other side of the river.

Sight Words

The sight words in this list are the words repeated throughout this trickster tale. You may decide to preview these for additional repetition before reading the readers' theater script together.

all	are	be	call	came	can	could	does	did	down	eight
fast	five	four	good	how	in	is	it	jump	know	live
many	must	not	of	one	other	seven	should	sing	the	the
six	small	ten	that	too	two	until	up	us		

Vocabulary Words

The words in this list may be new words for your students. Review the list before reading the readers' theater script with your students.

animal	count	crocodile	idea
jungle	mouse	river	tricksters

Characters

Narrator 1_____

Narrator 2_____

Mouse _____

Crocodile _____

All_____

Mouse Tricks the Crocodiles

Narrator 1: Mouse is the smallest animal. Mouse is small.

Narrator 2: Mouse is the smallest animal in the jungle. Mouse is small.

Mouse: I am the smallest in the jungle. I am small.

All: Mouse is the smallest animal. Mouse is small.

Narrator 1: Crocodile is the meanest animal. Crocodile is mean.

Narrator 2: Crocodile is the meanest animal in the jungle. Crocodile is mean.

Crocodile: I am the meanest in the jungle. I am mean.

All: Crocodile is the meanest animal. Crocodile is mean.

Narrator 1: One day, Mouse wanted to cross the river. Mouse is the smallest animal.

Narrator 2: Mouse could not cross the river. It was fast. It was strong. Mouse is the smallest animal.

Mouse: I cannot cross the river. It is too fast. It is too strong.

All: Mouse is the smallest animal. Mouse is small.

Narrator 1: Crocodile was in the river. It was fast. It was strong.

Narrator 2: Crocodile lives in the river. Crocodile is the meanest animal.

Crocodile: I live in the river. I like it fast. I like it strong.

All: Crocodile is the meanest animal. Crocodile is mean.

Narrator 1: Mouse had an idea. He called to the crocodiles from the bank of the river.

Narrator 2: Mouse had a very good idea. He told the crocodiles the king had given him an order.

Mouse Tricks the Crocodiles *(cont.)*

Mouse: Crocodiles in the fast, strong river, the king has given an order. The king has given an order.

Crocodile: What is the king's order, smallest animal of the jungle? What is the king's order, small mouse?

All: What is the king's order? What is the king's order?

Mouse: The king has given an order. The king orders that all the crocodiles in the river should be counted.

Crocodile: Why does the king give this order? Why must all the crocodiles in the river be counted?

Mouse: Crocodiles are the meanest animal in the jungle. The crocodiles live in the fast, strong river. The king orders the crocodiles to be counted. He wants to know how many of you live in the fast, strong river.

Crocodile: How will the king count all the mean crocodiles? How will he know how many of us live in the fast, strong river?

All: How will the king count all the mean crocodiles? How will he count them in the fast, strong river?

Narrator 1: Mouse had an idea. Mouse began to tell the crocodile to line up all the others in the fast, strong river.

Narrator 2: Mouse had a very good idea. Mouse told the crocodiles to line up. Line up in a row from one bank of the river to the other bank.

Mouse: Call all the crocodiles in the fast, strong river. Call them all to line up in a row.

Narrator 1: The crocodiles came to the river bank. Many, many crocodiles came to be counted.

Mouse Tricks the Crocodiles *(cont.)*

Narrator 2: The crocodiles lined up at the river bank. Many, many crocodiles lined up in a row.

Crocodile: All the crocodiles in the fast, strong river are here. We are all lined up in a row from one bank of the river to the other bank.

Narrator 1: Mouse had an idea. Mouse looked across the row of crocodiles to the other bank of the river.

Narrator 2: Mouse had a very good idea. Mouse hopped onto the back of crocodile.

Mouse: The king has given an order. The king has ordered that all the crocodiles be counted. ONE! TWO!

ALL: ONE! TWO! THREE! FOUR! FIVE! SIX! SEVEN! EIGHT! NINE! TEN!

Narrator 1: Mouse jumped across the crocodiles one by one counting out loud.

Mouse: ONE! TWO! THREE! FOUR! FIVE! SIX! SEVEN! EIGHT! NINE! TEN!

Narrator 2: Mouse is a trickster. Mouse jumped across the crocodiles until he reached the other bank.

Mouse: Crocodile, I am the smallest in the jungle. And you are the meanest in the jungle. I have tricked you to get to the other side of the river. You are mean but you are not smart.

All: Mouse is the smallest in the jungle. But Mouse had a very good idea.

Mouse Tricks the Crocodiles *(cont.)*

Character Mask for Mouse

Mouse Tricks the Crocodiles *(cont.)*

Character Mask for Crocodile

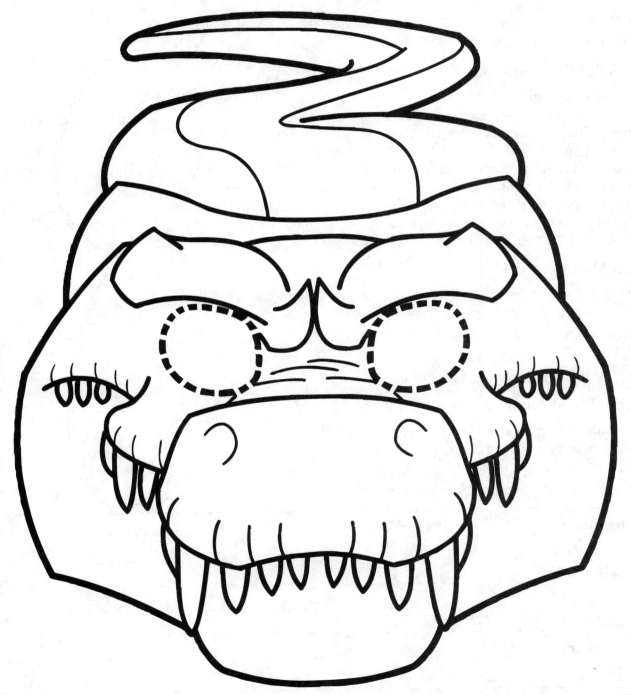

The Tiger, the Elephant, and the Mouse

Roles

Narrator 1 & 2, Tiger, Mouse, Elephant, All

Trickster Tale Summary

This tale sounds much like the classic Henny Penny story. The tiger is the trickster of this tale. He manages to fool both the elephant and the mouse. The tiger falls into a deep pit in the jungle and is unable to jump out on his own. His clever idea for getting out of the hole is to have other jungle creatures join him in the hole so that he can climb out. He tells the mouse that he is hiding in the hole because he has heard that the sky is going to fall. He will be safe down in the hole and the mouse, of course, runs off to tell the rest of the jungle creatures of the impending disaster. The elephant is the only other creature that believes this "whopper" and goes into the pit with the tiger and the mouse. The tiger jumps onto the back of the elephant and gets out of the hole. The mouse and the elephant are foolishly stuck down in the pit.

Sight Words

The sight words in this list are the words repeated throughout this trickster tale.

a	about	all	and	are	at	away	back	be	but	by	came
can	could	day	did	do	down	fall	has	have	he	here	how
I	in	into	is	it	jump	new	not	of	off	out	sat
see	that	the	then	there	walk	we	what	will	you		

Vocabulary Words

The words in this list may be new words for your students. Review the list before reading the readers' theater script with your students.

elephant	giraffe	laugh	jungle	monkey	
mouse	safe	tiger	thought	trickster	worried

Characters

Narrator 1 _____

Narrator 2 _____

Tiger _____

Mouse _____

Elephant _____

All _____

The Tiger, the Elephant, and the Mouse

Narrator 1: Tiger walks in the jungle. Tiger walks here and there in the jungle.

Narrator 2: One day as Tiger walked here and there in the jungle, he fell. He fell into a deep hole.

Tiger: I have fallen into a deep hole. I can not climb out of this deep hole. I can not jump out of the deep hole.

Narrator 1: Tiger could not climb out of the deep hole.

Narrator 2: Tiger could not jump out of the deep hole.

Tiger: What will I do? I can not climb out. I can not jump out.

Narrator 1: Tiger sat and thought about how to get out of the deep hole. He thought and he thought and he thought.

Narrator 2: Tiger sat and thought. Then Mouse came by the deep hole.

Mouse: Tiger, what are you doing? What are you doing down in that deep hole?

Tiger: Mouse, I have news. I have news that the sky is going to fall.

Mouse: Tiger, you have news that the sky is going to fall?

Tiger: Yes, I have news that the sky is going to fall. The sky will fall on all animals in the jungle.

Mouse: Is it true? Will the sky fall on all the animals in the jungle?

Tiger: Yes, it is true. The sky will fall and I will be safe down in this deep hole.

Mouse: I see that the deep hole is safe. I must tell the other animals so that they can be safe. I must tell them that the sky is going to fall.

The Tiger, the Elephant, and the Mouse *(cont.)*

Narrator 1: Mouse ran off to tell the other animals. He told the other animals that the sky was going to fall.

Narrator 2: Mouse ran off and told Monkey the sky was going to fall. Mouse ran off and told Giraffe the sky was going to fall. Mouse ran off and told Elephant the sky was going to fall.

Mouse: Monkey, Monkey, it is true. It is true. Tiger has news that the sky is going to fall.

All: Monkey laughed at Mouse.

Mouse: Giraffe, Giraffe, it is true. It is true. Tiger has news that the sky is going to fall.

All: Giraffe laughed at Mouse.

Mouse: Elephant, Elephant, it is true. It is true. Tiger has news that the sky is going to fall.

Narrator 1: Elephant did not laugh at Mouse. Elephant was very worried.

Elephant: Is it true? Does Tiger have news that the sky is going to fall?

Mouse: Yes, it is true. Tiger will be safe down in the deep hole. Tiger will be safe. We can be safe.

Elephant: We will be safe in the deep hole.

Narrator 2: Mouse and Elephant went to the deep hole. Tiger sat in the deep hole and could not climb out. He could not jump out.

Elephant: Tiger, is it true? Is the sky going to fall?

Tiger: Elephant, yes, it is true. The sky is going to fall on all the animals. But I will be safe in this deep hole.

Elephant: I want to be safe. Mouse wants to be safe. Can we come into the deep hole to be safe?

The Tiger, the Elephant, and the Mouse *(cont.)*

Tiger: Yes, Elephant. You can be safe. Mouse can be safe. The sky will not fall on you in this deep hole.

Narrator 1: Elephant jumped into the deep hole.

Narrator 2: Mouse jumped into the deep hole.

All: Tiger, Elephant, and Mouse were all in the deep hole.

Narrator 1: Tiger is a trickster. Tiger could not climb out of the deep hole. Tiger could not jump out of the hole.

Narrator 2: Elephant could not climb out of the deep hole. Elephant could not jump out of the deep hole.

Narrator 1: Mouse could not climb out of the deep hole. Mouse could not jump out of the deep hole.

Narrator 2: Tiger jumped on the back of Elephant. Tiger jumped from the back of Elephant out of the deep hole.

Tiger: Elephant and Mouse, you will be safe in the deep hole.

Narrator 1: Tiger left Elephant and Mouse in the deep hole. Elephant could not climb out of the deep hole. Mouse could not climb out of the deep hole.

Narrator 2: Tiger left Elephant and Mouse in the deep hole. Elephant could not jump out of the deep hole. Mouse could not jump out of the deep hole.

The Tiger, the Elephant, and the Mouse *(cont.)*

Character Mask for Tiger

The Tiger, the Elephant, and the Mouse *(cont.)*

Character Mask for Elephant

Coyote's Colorful Hat

Roles

Narrator 1 & 2, Coyote, Gecko, Turtle, All

Trickster Tale Summary

Coyote is the trickster in this tale. He has two very good friends both of whom he is a bit jealous. He gets a new hat which is two sided. One side is white and the other side is red. He tricks his friends into a 'knock down, drag out' fight with each other by starting an argument with his hat. One friend says it is a white hat. The other says that it is a red hat. Both, of course, are right, and coyote enjoys the argument.

Sight Words

The sight words in this list are the words repeated throughout this trickster tale.

a	away	but	color	good	has	here	friend	his	in	is
left	like	look	me	more	morning	my	new	no	on	one
over	put	red	right	see	show	so	soon	that	the	them
thing	to	two	very	walk	was	white	with			

Vocabulary Words

The words in this list may be new words for your students. Review the list before reading the readers' theater script with your students.

angry	coyote	decided	fight	gecko
laughing	proud	tricked	trickster	turtle

Characters

Narrator 1 _____

Narrator 2 _____

Coyote _____

Gecko _____

Turtle _____

All _____

Coyote's Colorful Hat

Narrator 1: Coyote has two good friends. Coyote is a good friend to Turtle. Coyote is a good friend with Gecko. Coyote has two good friends.

Narrator 2: Turtle has two good friends. Turtle is a good friend to Gecko. Turtle is a good friend to Coyote. Turtle has two good friends.

Narrator 1: Gecko has two good friends. Gecko is a good friend to Turtle. Gecko is a good friend to Coyote. Gecko has two good friends.

All: Coyote and Turtle and Gecko are good friends.

Coyote: Turtle is my good friend. Gecko is my good friend.

Turtle: Gecko is my good friend. Coyote is my good friend.

Gecko: Coyote is my good friend. Turtle is my good friend.

Narrator 2: One morning Coyote put on a new hat. Coyote put on a new hat that was white on one side. Coyote put on a new hat that was red on one side. Coyote's new hat was red and white.

Narrator 1: Coyote went walking in his new hat. Coyote went walking in his red and white hat. Coyote went walking to see his two good friends.

Coyote: I am going to show Turtle my hat. I am going to show Gecko my hat. I want my two good friends to see my red and white hat.

All: Coyote went walking in his new red and white hat.

Narrator 1: Gecko and Turtle met Coyote on the road. They met Coyote in his new hat. The good friends met on the road.

Narrator 2: But Coyote is a trickster. He decided to trick his good friends. Coyote is too proud of his fine hat. Coyote is too proud of his new red and white hat.

Turtle: Here is Coyote in a new hat. Here is Coyote looking very proud in his new hat.

Coyote's Colorful Hat *(cont.)*

Gecko: Here is Coyote in a new hat. Here is Coyote looking very proud in his new hat.

Turtle: Coyote is so proud of himself in his new hat. Coyote is going to walk right by me on the road!

Gecko: Coyote is so proud of himself in his new hat. Coyote is going to walk right by me on the road!

All: Coyote went walking in his new red and white hat. Coyote is too proud of his fine hat. Coyote is too proud of his fine hat.

Narrator 1: Gecko and Turtle sat on the side as Coyote walked right by them on the road. Gecko sat on the right side of the road. Turtle sat on the left side of the road. Coyote walked right by them on the road.

Narrator 2: Gecko saw Coyote walk by in his red hat. Gecko saw the new red hat. Gecko saw Coyote in his fine new hat.

Narrator 1: Turtle saw Coyote walk by in his white hat. Turtle saw the new white hat. Turtle saw Coyote in his fine new hat.

Gecko: What a fine new hat Coyote has on his head! What a fine red hat he has.

Turtle: What a fine new hat Coyote has on his head! What a fine white hat he has, my friend Gecko.

Gecko: It is a fine red hat, my friend Turtle!

Turtle: It is a fine white hat, my friend Gecko!

Gecko: No, it is red!

Turtle: No, it is white!

Gecko: Red!

Turtle: White!

Coyote's Colorful Hat *(cont.)*

Gecko:	**Red!**
Turtle:	**White!**
Gecko:	**Red!**
Turtle:	**White!**
Narrator 1:	Gecko and Turtle yelled loudly. Gecko and Turtle yelled louder.
Narrator 2:	Gecko and Turtle became angry. Gecko and Turtle became angrier and angrier.
All:	Gecko and Turtle yell. Gecko and Turtle are angry. But Gecko and Turtle are good friends.
Narrator 1:	Soon Gecko and Turtle are fighting and hitting. But Gecko and Turtle are good friends. They are fighting and hitting.
Narrator 2:	Gecko and Turtle are fighting and hitting. They are fighting and hitting about Coyote's new hat. But Gecko and Turtle are good friends.
Narrator 1:	But Coyote is a trickster. He decided to trick his good friends. Coyote is too proud of his fine hat. Coyote is too proud of his new red and white hat.
Narrator 2:	Coyote has tricked his friends. He has tricked them with his new red and white hat. He has tricked them into fighting and hitting.
Coyote:	Here is my hat. Here is my fine new hat. You are right, Gecko. My hat is red. See, it is a red hat on this side. And you are right, Turtle. My hat is white. See, it is a white hat on this side.
Gecko:	See, it is a red hat! See, Turtle! I am right.
Turtle:	See, it is a white hat! See, Gecko! I am right.
Gecko:	I am right!
Turtle:	I am right!

Coyote's Colorful Hat *(cont.)*

Gecko: No, I am!

Turtle: No, I am!

Gecko: No, I am!

Turtle: No, I am!

Gecko: No, I am!

Turtle: No, I am!

Narrator 1:   Coyote went away laughing at his two good friends. Coyote had tricked his two good friends.

Narrator 2:   Coyote tricked his two good friends into fighting over a silly thing like the color of his hat. Coyote has a fine red and white hat.

Coyote's Colorful Hat *(cont.)*

Character Mask for Coyote

Coyote's Colorful Hat (cont.)

Character Mask for Gecko

Coyote's Colorful Hat *(cont.)*

Character Mask for Turtle

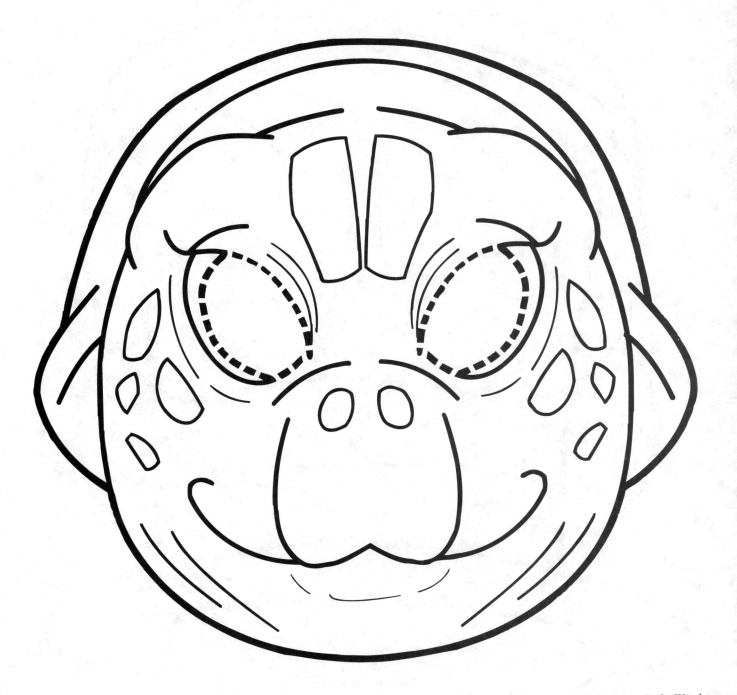

Coyote's Colorful Hat *(cont.)*

Pattern for Top Hat

Coyote and Hen

Roles

Narrator 1 & 2, Hen & Coyote, All

Trickster Tale Summary

In this tale, the trickster is tricked! Coyote tries to persuade the hen to come out of the tree so that he can eat her as dinner. He tells her that they now have made a peace treaty together. But suspecting that the coyote was up to his same old trickery, she tells the coyote that the dog is coming to make peace with the coyote. Since the dog and the hen have not made peace, she is afraid to come down out of the tree. And the dog and coyote have not made peace either. The coyote runs away, afraid of an encounter with the dog. Of course, the hen is left alone in the tree in peace!

Sight Words

The sight words in this list are the words repeated throughout this trickster tale.

about	am	are	away	because	call	came	come	could	do	dog
down	for	friend	from	good	have	he	hear	how	I	in
is	it	know	made	news	not	of	on	out	other	ran
see	some	tell	the	there	to	too	two	tree	up	us
want	we	what	where	will	with	you				

Vocabulary Words

The words in this list may be new words for your students. Review the list before reading the readers' theater script with your students.

afraid	coyote	everything	hurry	mountain
peace	treaty	trickster	truth	watches

Characters

Narrator 1 _____

Narrator 2 _____

Hen _____

Coyote _____

Coyote and Hen

Narrator 1:   Hen is up in the tree. Hen watches everything from up in the tree. Hen sees Coyote come up to the tree.

All: Hen watches everything from up in the tree.

Narrator 2:   Coyote came up to the tree. Coyote called out to hen up in the tree.

All: Hen watches everything from up in the tree.

Coyote: Hen, I have some good news for you. Do you want to hear it? I have good news.

All: Watch out, Hen! Coyote is a trickster! Watch out, Hen!

Narrator 1:   Hen is up in the tree. Hen watches everything from up in the tree.

Hen: Do you really have some good news, Coyote? Do you have good news?

Coyote: It is about the two of us. It is about Coyote and Hen.

Hen: What good news could you have about Coyote and Hen?

Narrator 2:   Coyote called out to Hen up in the tree.

Coyote: Coyote and Hen have made peace. It is good news. We are friends now. Come down from the tree. We are friends.

All: Watch out, Hen! Coyote is a trickster! Watch out, Hen!

Hen: It is good news, Coyote. Where is the peace treaty? How do I know the peace is real? Where is the peace treaty? How do I know the peace is real?

Coyote: It is there. Over there on the other side of the mountain. Hurry and come down! Hurry and come down!

Hen: Over there on the other side of the mountain? Where on the other side of the mountain?

Coyote: Over there on the other side of the mountain. Hurry and come down! Hurry and come down!

Coyote and Hen *(cont.)*

Hen: How do I know the peace is real? Where is the peace treaty? How do I know the peace is real?

Coyote: Over there on the other side of the mountain. Hurry and come down! Hurry and come down! I am telling the truth. Come down from the tree.

Hen: Maybe you are telling the truth. Maybe you are not telling the truth.

Coyote: I am telling the truth. I am telling the truth.

All: Watch out, Hen! Coyote is a trickster! Watch out, Hen!

Hen: I see Dog coming. I see Dog coming from up in the tree. He is coming because you and he are going to make peace, too.

Coyote: Dog is coming? You see him coming? Do you hear him coming, too?

All: Watch out, Hen! Coyote is a trickster! Watch out, Hen!

Hen: I see Dog coming. I hear Dog coming. He is coming fast. He is coming to make peace, too! I can not come down because dog will grab me.

Narrator 1: Coyote did not see Dog coming. He did not hear Dog coming. And Coyote had not made peace with Dog.

Narrator 2: Coyote had not made peace with Dog. Coyote was afraid of Dog. Coyote ran away as fast as he could.

Narrator 1: Hen did not see Dog coming. But Hen knew that Coyote had not made peace with Dog. She knew he was not telling the truth.

Narrator 2: Hen knew that Coyote is a trickster. Hen knew he would grab her if she came down from the tree. Hen tricked the trickster, Coyote!

Coyote and Hen *(cont.)*

Character Mask for Hen

Bluebird and Weasel

Roles

Narrator 1 & 2, Bluebird, Weasel

Trickster Tale Summary

The bluebird has not always been a beautiful blue. This tale describes how the bluebird gets his beautiful color and tricks the weasel as well. The bluebird bathes and sings in the blue water of the lake four times a day. On the fourth day, his feathers disappear only to reappear on the fifth day in a beautiful shade of blue. Weasel watches this and envies the color of the bluebird. Following the bluebird's directions, the weasel also bathes four times a day for four days in the blue water of the lake. He also gets a beautiful blue color but stumbles and rolls in the dust. His blue color becomes the dull color of the dust.

Sight Word List

The sight words in this list are the words repeated throughout this trickster tale.

a	all	again	am	and	any	are	at	be	brown	but
by	came	color	come	day	did	eat	four	he	here	how
I	in	into	is	it	jump	live	look	love	morning	much
left	like	now	of	on	once	out	pretty	sing	so	
such	than	that	the	there	they	to	too	upon	very	
walk	want	was	water	where	while	with	would			

Vocabulary Word List

The words in this list may be new words for your students. Review the list before reading the readers' theater script with your students.

afraid	blue	bird	everyone	feathers	fourth	lake	proud
supper	tasty	vain	watched	weasel	without	yahoo	

Characters

Narrator 1 _____

Narrator 2 _____

Bluebird _____

Weasel _____

Bluebird and Weasel

Narrator 1: Once upon a time, Bluebird was a very dull brown color. Bluebird was dull. Bluebird was brown.

Narrator 2: Once upon a time, Bluebird lived by a lake. Bluebird lived by a lake with clear blue water.

Narrator 1: Bluebird loved the blue of the water in the lake. The lake was so clear and so blue. Bluebird loved it.

Narrator 2: Bluebird loved the blue of the water in the lake so much that he washed in the lake. Bluebird loved it.

Narrator 1: Bluebird loved the blue of the water so much he washed in the lake four times a day.

Narrator 2: Bluebird loved the blue water of the lake so much he would sing while he washed.

Bluebird: *(sung to the tune of Are You Sleeping?)*

> There is blue water.
> There is blue water
> It is here.
> It is here.
> I went in.
> I went in.
> I am blue.
> I am blue.

Narrator 1: Bluebird would sing while he washed. He washed in the lake four times a day. Four times a day he sang his song.

Bluebird: *(sung to the tune of Are You Sleeping?)*

> There is blue water.
> There is blue water
> It is here.
> It is here.
> I went in.
> I went in.
> I am blue.
> I am blue.

Bluebird and Weasel *(cont.)*

Narrator 1: Weasel watched Bluebird wash in the lake. Weasel hid and watched Bluebird.

Narrator 2: Weasel watched Bluebird. Weasel wanted to eat Bluebird for supper. Weasel is afraid of the water.

Weasel: Bluebird would be a tasty supper. I would like to catch Bluebird for supper. But I am afraid of the water.

Narrator 1: Bluebird would sing while he washed. He washed in the lake four times a day. Four times a day he sang his song.

Narrator 2: On the fourth morning, Bluebird came out of the blue water. He came out of the lake without any feathers at all. Bluebird came out of the blue water bare.

Bluebird: Where are my feathers? Where have my feathers gone? I have come out of the blue water bare!

Narrator 1: On the fifth morning, Bluebird came out of the blue water. He came out of the lake with blue feathers. Bluebird came out of the water blue.

Bluebird: Here are my feathers. Here they are and they are pretty blue feathers.

Weasel: How did the dull brown color of your feathers come out? You are all blue now. How did you make the brown come out?

Bluebird: I went in the blue water of the lake. I washed in the water four times a day.

Weasel: Your feathers are such a pretty blue. You are as blue as the water in the lake. You are prettier than any bird that flies in the air. You are prettier than any bird that swims on the lake.

Bluebird: I went in the blue water of the lake. I washed in the water four times a day. I sang a song each time I went into the blue water in the lake.

Weasel: I want to be a pretty blue. I want to be a pretty blue, too.

Bluebird and Weasel (cont.)

Narrator 1: So, bluebird sang his song for the weasel. Bluebird sang.

Bluebird: *(sung to the tune of Are you Sleeping?)*

There is blue water.

There is blue water

It is here.

It is here.

I went in.

I went in.

I am blue.

I am blue.

Narrator 2: Weasel wanted to be a pretty blue, too. Weasel sang the song too. He sang along with Bluebird.

Weasel & *(sung to the tune of Are You Sleeping?)*

Bluebird: There is blue water

There is blue water

It is here.

It is here.

I went in.

I went in.

I am blue.

I am blue.

Narrator 1: Weasel sang along with Bluebird and then jumped into the lake. Weasel is afraid of the water but he still jumped into the lake.

Narrator 2: Weasel sang Bluebird's song. Weasel sang as he jumped into the lake. Weasel sang and bathed like Bluebird four times a day.

Narrator 1: Weasel sang and washed like Bluebird four times a day. On the fifth day, he came out of the water as blue as Bluebird. Weasel was now a pretty blue, too.

Bluebird and Weasel *(cont.)*

Weasel: *(sung to the tune of Are You Sleeping?)*

There is blue water.

There is blue water

It is here.

It is here.

I went in.

I went in.

I am blue.

I am blue.

I am really blue. I am a pretty, pretty blue. Yahoo!

Bluebird: Why, Weasel! It is true! You are really blue. You are a pretty, pretty blue.

Narrator 2: Weasel became very proud. Weasel became very vain. He wanted everyone to see him. He wanted everyone to see his pretty, pretty blue fur.

Narrator 1: Weasel looked left. Weasel looked right because he wanted everyone to see his pretty, pretty blue fur.

Narrator 2: Weasel was not watching where he was walking. Weasel looked left. Weasel looked right. Watch out, you weasel!

Narrator 1: Weasel ran into a stump. Weasel rolled and rolled on the ground. When weasel got up again, he was the color of the dust.

Narrator 2: Weasel was not blue. Weasel was not a pretty, pretty blue. Weasel was the color of dust. To this day, Weasel is the color of dust.

Bluebird and Weasel *(cont.)*

Character Mask for Weasel

Bluebird and Weasel *(cont.)*

Character Mask for Bluebird

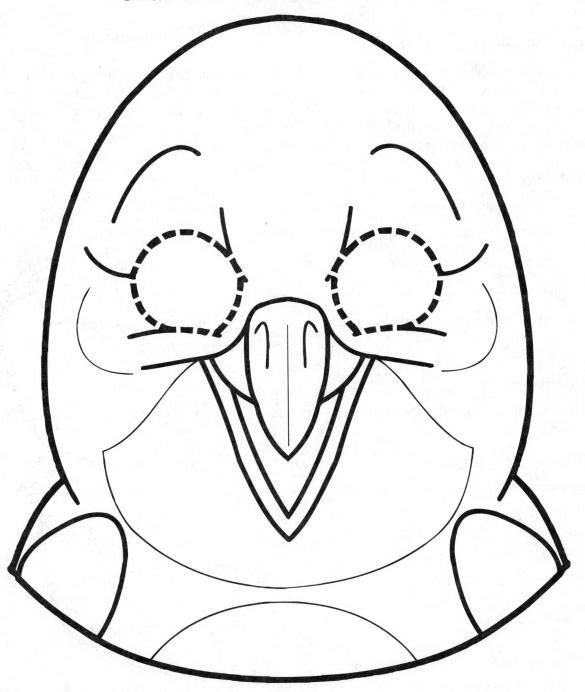

Eagle Takes the Moon

Roles

Narrator 1& 2, Eagle, All

Trickster Tale Summary

This version of an ancient Native American creation myth has the eagle in the trickster role. Eagle is the trickster character who takes pity on the people in darkness and goes looking for a light. Eagle finds a ball of light at the edge of the world. However, it is guarded in a box so eagle must trick a little girl into allowing him to get to the ball of light. He plays with the girl and is allowed to play with the ball of light, and then steals it to place in the sky for the people in darkness.

Sight Words

The sight words in this list are the words repeated throughout this trickster tale.

a	about	again	and	any	away	be	boy	ball	big	box
call	color	down	every	far	for	girl	happy	he	him	I
in	it	into	little	look	made	many	me	more	not	open
of	put	people	play	pretty	so	small	the	they	tree	to
up	was	were	will	with	where	water				

Vocabulary Words

The words in this list may be new words for your students. Review the list before reading the readers' theater script with your students.

edge	glowing	eagle	earth	watch

Characters

Narrator 1_____

Narrator 2_____

Eagle _____

All _____

Eagle Takes the Moon *(cont.)*

Narrator 1:   The earth is dark. It is dark.

Narrator 2:   The sky is dark. It is dark.

All: It is dark. It is night.

Narrator 1:   The waters are dark. They are dark.

Narrator 2:   The people are in the dark. They are in the dark. It is always night.

All: They are in the dark. It is always night.

Narrator 1:   It is dark and night. Dark and night.

Narrator 2:   Eagle flies in the sky. He sees that it is dark and cold.

Eagle: I am sad for the people. It is dark and night. It is always night

All: It is dark and night. It is always night.

Eagle: I will look for light for the people. I will look for light.

Narrator 1:   Eagle flies to look for light. It is dark everywhere he flies.

Narrator 2:   Eagle looks for light down. Eagle looks for light up. He looked up and down for light.

All: Up and down. Up and Down. It is dark everywhere.

Narrator 1:   Eagle sees a bit of light. He sees light far, far away.

Narrator 2:   Eagle flies to the light. He flies close to the light.

All: Eagle sees a bit of light. It is far, far away. Eagle flies to the light.

Eagle: The light is at the end of the earth.

Narrator 1:   The light is in a house. The light is shining.

All: The light is shining. The light is shining in a house.

Eagle Takes the Moon *(cont.)*

Narrator 2: Eagle flies to the house. Eagle watches. He watches the shining light.

All: Eagle watches the house. Eagle watches the shining light.

Narrator 1: Eagle watches a pretty little girl come out of the house.

Narrator 2: Eagle watches the pretty little girl at the edge of the world.

All: Eagle watches the house. Eagle watches the shining light. Eagle watches the little girl.

Narrator 1: Eagle watches the pretty little girl. She goes to the edge of the world.

Narrator 2: Eagle wants to be with the pretty little girl.

All: Eagle watches the girl. Eagle wants to be with the pretty little girl.

Narrator 1: Eagle flies to the edge of the world. Eagle flies to the pretty little girl.

Narrator 2: The pretty little girl plays with Eagle.   Eagle and the pretty little girl play at the edge of the world.

Narrator 1: Eagle goes into the house to watch the pretty little girl. Eagle goes into the house to play with the pretty little girl.

Narrator 2: Eagle goes into the house to play with the pretty little girl. Eagle looks for the light as he plays.

Narrator 2: Eagle looks for the light. Eagle plays with the pretty little girl. Eagle sees a big box in the house.

Eagle Takes the Moon *(cont.)*

All: Eagle finds a big box. Eagle finds a big box in the house.

Narrator 1: The pretty little girl places the box in front of Eagle.

Narrator 2: The pretty little girl opens the lid of the box.

Eagle: Inside the box is a smaller box. Inside that box is an even smaller box.

Narrator 1: Inside the smallest box is a glowing ball.

Narrator 2: Light pours out of the smallest box. Light pours out of the glowing ball.

All: Light pours out of the glowing ball.

Narrator 1: The pretty little girl gives Eagle the glowing ball to play with. Light pours out of the glowing ball.

Narrator 2: Light pours out of the ball. Eagle plays with the glowing ball. Eagle rolls the glowing ball.

All: Light pours out of the glowing ball.

Eagle: I will take the glowing ball back to the people in the dark.

Narrator 1: Eagle is a trickster. Eagle snaps up the glowing ball. Eagle flies away from the edge of the earth.

Narrator 2: Eagle is a trickster. Eagle flies away with the glowing ball. Eagle flies to the people in the dark.

All: Eagle flies away from the edge of the earth. Eagle flies to the people in the dark. Eagle flies with the glowing ball.

Eagle Takes the Moon *(cont.)*

Eagle: I will put the glowing ball up in the sky. I will put the glowing ball above the people in the dark. Light will pour out of the glowing ball.

Narrator 1: Eagle placed the glowing ball high up in the sky. Light poured out of the glowing ball.

Narrator 2: Eagle took the moon. Night is not dark. Light pours out of the glowing ball.

Narrator 1: Eagle took the moon. Eagle put the moon up in the sky.

All: Eagle took the moon. Eagle put the moon up in the sky. Night is not dark.

Eagle Takes the Moon *(cont.)*

Character Mask for Eagle

Spider Catches the Snake

Roles

Narrator 1 & 2, Tiger, Spider, Snake, All

Trickster Tale Summary

The trickster of this tale is the smallest jungle creature, the spider. No one suspects him of trickery until one day when he wants to have the same privileges as the king of the jungle, the ferocious tiger. The spider wants to name something in the jungle after himself as the tiger does. The tiger agrees on one condition. The spider must tie up the frightening snake. Spider devises a trick to have the snake tie himself up and shows the tiger that the itsy bitsy spider outwits even the scariest jungle creature.

Sight Words

The sight words in this list are the words repeated throughout this trickster tale.

a	at	after	all	and	ask	by	can	call	day	do
first	goes	give	have	head	him	his	home	how	hot	I
is	it	in	let	long	like	me	must	my	name	no
not	now	of	on	one	please	pretty	put	said	see	shall
should	show	she	stops	so	the	than	that	then	there	thinks
this	to	too	tree	under	up	walks	went	will	would	you

Vocabulary Words

The words in this list may be new words for your students. Review the list before reading the readers' theater script with your students.

flower	bitsy	itsy	jungle	laugh
limps	spider	snake	stretch	

Characters

Narrator 1 _____

Narrator 2 _____

Tiger _____

Spider _____

Snake _____

All _____

Spider Catches the Snake

Narrator 1: Spider limps in the jungle. No one sees itsy, bitsy Spider. No one thinks of itsy, bitsy Spider.

All: No one sees itsy, bitsy Spider. No one thinks of itsy, bitsy Spider.

Narrator 2: Tiger walks in the jungle. Tiger walks here and there in the jungle. Tiger is king in the jungle.

All: Tiger is king in the jungle. Tiger is king in the jungle.

Narrator 1: One day, Spider stops under a pretty flower. It is so hot. Spider is under the pretty flower. Then Tiger walks by.

Narrator 2: Spider said nothing. Spider was under the pretty flower when Tiger walks by. Tiger stops near the pretty flower. Spider said nothing.

All: Spider said nothing. Spider said nothing.

Tiger: I will call this flower a "tiger lily." I will give this flower my name. I am king in the jungle.

Narrator 1: Spider said nothing. Spider was under the pretty flower when tiger walked by. Tiger is king in the jungle. Tiger can give the flower his name.

Narrator 2: Spider limps in the jungle. No one sees itsy, bitsy Spider. No one thinks of itsy, bitsy Spider. Everywhere the Spider limps, Spider finds Tiger's name.

All: No one sees itsy, bitsy Spider. No one thinks of itsy, bitsy Spider.

Spider: I would like something named after me. I want my name on something. Something in the jungle should have my name.

Narrator 1: Spider went to Tiger. Spider asked Tiger to name something after him.

Spider Catches the Snake *(cont.)*

Narrator 2: Spider went to Tiger. Spider said something should have his name.

All: No one sees itsy, bitsy Spider. No one thinks of itsy, bitsy Spider.

Spider: Tiger, please let me put my name on something. Please name something after me.

Tiger: (*laughing at the little spider*) Ha Ha! Spider, you can put your name on something. You can have something named after you.

Spider: Tiger, please let me put my name on something. Please name something after me.

Tiger: But first, you must tie up Snake. Then, you can name something after you.

All: No one sees itsy, bitsy Spider. No one thinks of itsy, bitsy Spider.

Narrator 1: Tiger is very afraid of Snake. Snake is afraid of Elephant. Spider is not afraid at all.

All: No one sees itsy, bitsy Spider. No one thinks of itsy, bitsy Spider.

Narrator 2: Spider thinks and thinks. He thinks up a plan.

Spider: I can not tie up Snake. But I am not afraid of Snake. I will wait.

Narrator 1: Spider waits and waits. He waits on his plan.

All: Spider waits and waits. He waits on his plan.

Narrator 2: Snake laughs and laughs. She learns that Spider is going to tie her up. Snake laughs and laughs.

All: Spider waits and waits. He waits on his plan.

Spider Catches the Snake *(cont.)*

Snake: (*laughing at the little spider*) Ha! Ha! Spider thinks he can tie me up!

All: Spider waits and waits. He waits on his plan.

Narrator 1: Finally, Snake can not wait any more. Snake goes to Spider's home. Snake goes to Spider.

Snake: (*laughing at the little spider*) Ha! Ha! Spider, do you think you can tie me up?

Spider: I can not tie you up, Snake. I shall show Tiger I can not tie you up.

Snake: How shall you do this, Spider? How shall you do this?

Spider: I shall show Tiger you are too long to tie up.

Snake: How shall you do this, Spider? How shall you do this?

Spider: I shall show Tiger you are longer than that tree. I shall show Tiger you are too long to tie up.

Snake: How shall you do this, Spider? How shall you do this?

Spider: Stretch yourself up the tree. Then I can see if you are longer than that tree.

Narrator 1: Snake stretched and stretched. He stretched and stretched himself up the tree.

Snake: See! I am longer than the tree. See! I am longer than the tree.

Spider: I can not see if you are longer than the tree. Tie your tail to the tree. Stretch yourself up the tree. Then I can see if you are longer than that tree.

Narrator 2: Snake tied his tail to the tree. Snake stretched and stretched. He stretched and stretched himself up the tree.

Snake: See! I am longer than the tree. See! I am longer than the tree.

Spider Catches the Snake *(cont.)*

Spider: I can not see if you are longer than the tree. Tie your head to the tree. Stretch yourself up the tree. Then I can see if you are longer than that tree.

Narrator 1: Snake tied his head to the tree. Snake stretched and stretched. He stretched and stretched himself up the tree.

Snake: See! I am longer than the tree. See! I am longer than the tree.

Spider: I can not see if you are longer than the tree. Let me tie you in the middle to the tree. Stretch yourself up the tree. Then I can see if you are longer than that tree.

Narrator 2: Snake let Spider tie his middle to the tree. Snake stretched and stretched. He stretched and stretched himself up the tree.

Snake: See! I am longer than the tree. See! I am longer than the tree. Now cut me free from the tree.

Spider: Ha! Ha! I am not afraid of Snake. See, Snake is tied up to the tree. Snake is tied up to the tree.

Narrator 1: No one sees itsy, bitsy Spider. No one thinks of itsy, bitsy Spider. Spider has tied up Snake to the tree.

All: No one sees itsy, bitsy Spider. No one thinks of itsy, bitsy Spider at all.

Spider Catches the Snake *(cont.)*

Character Mask for Spider

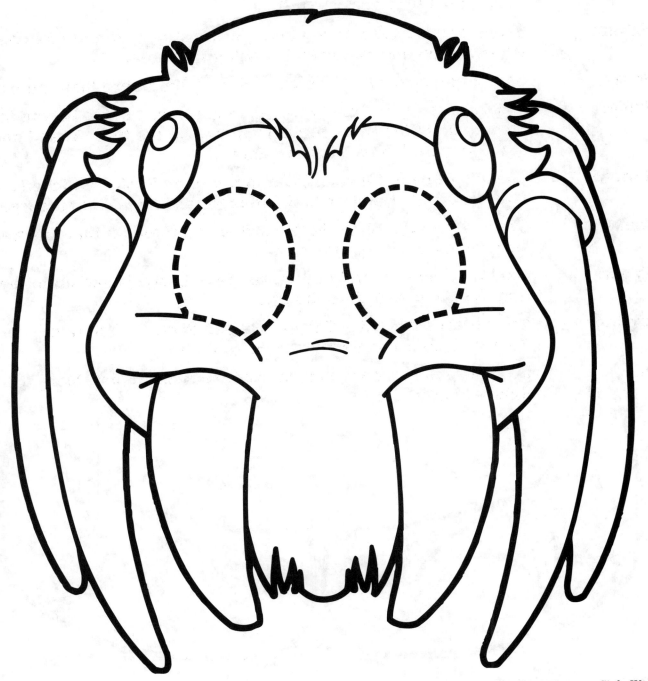

Spider Catches the Snake *(cont.)*

Character Mask for Snake

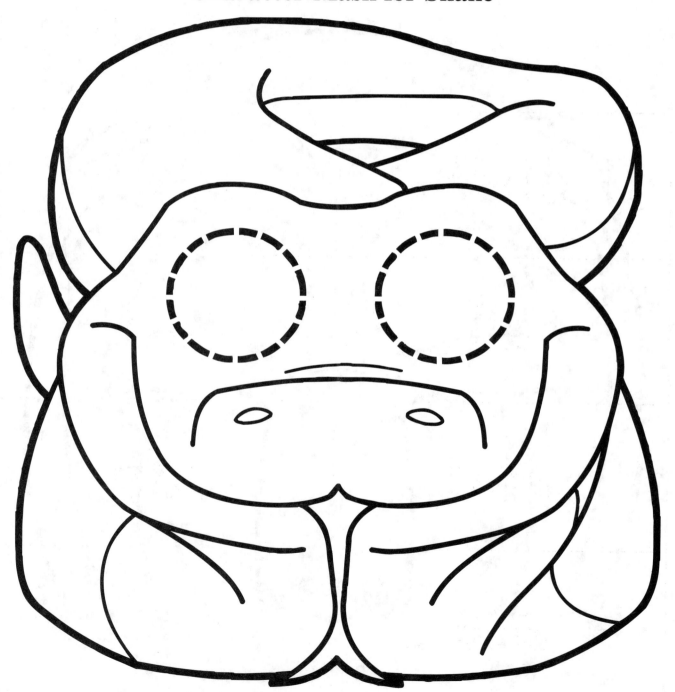

Sight Word Flashcards

a	about
after	again
all	am
and	any
are	at

Sight Word Flashcards *(cont.)*

as	ask
away	be
because	back
ball	big
box	brown

Sight Word Flashcards *(cont.)*

boy	but
call	came
can	color
could	close
cold	day

Sight Word Flashcards *(cont.)*

did	do
does	don't
down	eat
eight	every
fall	far

Sight Word Flashcards *(cont.)*

fast	find
fine	first
five	friend
for	four
fly	found

Sight Word Flashcards (cont.)

funny	get
girl	give
good	got
goes	have
he	here

Sight Word Flashcards *(cont.)*

him	his
hat	happy
head	hear
help	hot
house	how

Sight Word Flashcards *(cont.)*

here	help
I	if
in	is
it	into
jump	know

Sight Word Flashcards *(cont.)*

knew	like
little	line
leave	left
let	letters
live	long

Sight Word Flashcards *(cont.)*

look	love
me	my
many	may
much	more
must	made

Sight Word Flashcards *(cont.)*

morning	name
no	not
now	of
off	old
on	one

Sight Word Flashcards *(cont.)*

or	other
only	open
over	once
order	our
people	play

Sight Word Flashcards *(cont.)*

please	put
pretty	sat
some	see
shall	saw
said	stop

Sight Word Flashcards *(cont.)*

should	soon
seven	so
sing	six
small	show

Sight Word Flashcards (cont.)

that	the
their	them
then	there
they	this

Sight Word Flashcards *(cont.)*

three	to
too	tree
two	ten
thank	took

Sight Word Flashcards *(cont.)*

up	us
under	until
upon	very
was	we

Sight Word Flashcards *(cont.)*

were	what
will	with
want	walk
water	why

Sight Word Flashcards *(cont.)*

would	where
white	wash
went	you
such	tell

Sight Word Flashcards *(cont.)*

thing	thinks
than	she
while	